By Light and Hidden Matter

By Light and Hidden Matter

LYNNE GOLDSMITH

RESOURCE *Publications* · Eugene, Oregon

BY LIGHT AND HIDDEN MATTER

Copyright © 2022 Lynne Goldsmith. All rights reserved. Except for brief quotations in critical publications or reviews, no part of this book may be reproduced in any manner without prior written permission from the publisher. Write: Permissions, Wipf and Stock Publishers, 199 W. 8th Ave., Suite 3, Eugene, OR 97401.

Resource Publications
An Imprint of Wipf and Stock Publishers
199 W. 8th Ave., Suite 3
Eugene, OR 97401

www.wipfandstock.com

PAPERBACK ISBN: 978-1-6667-5960-0
HARDCOVER ISBN: 978-1-6667-5961-7
EBOOK ISBN: 978-1-6667-5962-4

10/13/22

For Every Rock, Plant, Forest, Creature, and Life Beyond

CONTENTS

ROCK

Tor | 3
Scree | 4
Mountain Ice: Snow Pack | 5
Sierra Nevada: Volcanic Arc, Inactive Subduction Zone | 6

PLANT

Plant Strategy | 11
Circumnutation | 12
Meristem | 13
Sounds of Vibration | 14
Boquila Trifoliolata in Chilean Rainforest | 16
Queen of the Andes, Puya Raimondii | 18
Endangered Frisco Clover | 19
Moss | 20
Anabiosis: Return to the Living | 21
Reviver: Fireweed | 22

FOREST

Lodgepole Pine Cone Touched by Fire | 25
The Silencing of Forests | 27
Mother Tree | 28
The Intelligence of Trees | 29
Outdoor Conversations | 30
Fairy Ring Fungi | 31
Textural Triangle | 32

CONTENTS

CREATURE: PART I

The Bleaching of Coral Reefs, AKA Polyp Animals | 37
Head Rearrangement | 38
Bodacious | 39
Operation Egglifts | 42
Ice Ecoregions: Reflections of White Bear | 45

CREATURE: PART II

Footprints, Bobcat, Fresh Snow | 49
Birds at Bayside | 50
Chickadee | 51
Crab Shells | 53
Butterfly | 54
Brotherhood | 55
Elephant Sisterhood | 56

MIGRATION

Diel Vertical Migration | 59
Migrations of Sea Turtles | 61
Red Crab Migration | 62
Pacific Salmon Run | 63
Migration: Monarch Butterfly | 65
Repose | 67
Migratory Flight of the Bar-Tailed Godwit | 68

MIRACLES, MORE

Water Bears | 73
DMS | 75
Immortality | 76

Fractal Reminders | 77

Fibonacci Series from Indian Mathematicians | 78

Hemimastigote (AKA Hairy, Rapacious Ogre) | 80

Subterranean Biosphere | 81

OUTER SPACE

Golden Nebula | 85

Arms of the Milky Way Holding Stars | 86

Milky Way's Black Hole | 87

Star Consumed | 88

Neutron Star Revived | 89

Binary System: White Dwarf Accompanying Red Giant | 90

Reflection Nebula | 91

Dark Matter | 92

Acknowledgments | 93

List of Abbreviations | 95

ROCK

TOR

You are what's left behind:
pillows of rock worn,
joints defined,
topsoil gone

after pressure release,
freeze-thaw,
chemical weathering
has taken your sides

their joints close enough
to fall away into scree
to happen again
is just a matter of time.

SCREE

From cliff face, rock falls
to an angle of repose

for suiting itself.
Rubble waits

for more of shaking up,
ice within mountain slopes,

water freezing
to make new cracks

maybe even to break rocks.
Either way, however it happens,

cliff degrades
through stressors:

biotic, chemical,
thermal, topographic.

Glacier to be covered.
Scree to layer,

slope to become mantled.
Burying occurs at all levels.

MOUNTAIN ICE: SNOW PACK

Freeze-thaw bursts the rocks.
Rotational shift occurs.

Above the glacier, scree falls
to debris below on valley floor.

Rocks scrape and scour.
Plucking occurs (rocks breaking off)

creating steep back walls (mountainside)
with armchair-shaped hollow.

Glacier moves through corrie
down into U-shaped valley.

Interlocking spurs crashed through,
moraine working. Tarns formed above
in corrie

with erratic stones settling below
in glacial trough.

Ice melted
thousands of years ago—
Last Age of Ice.

SIERRA NEVADA: VOLCANIC ARC, INACTIVE SUBDUCTION ZONE

Through magma chambers cooled I walk
over Jurassic stone, batholith, granite
that rose—may have—

plutons from underground
formed 200 million years ago

to be eroded now, into peaks,
sliding plates done, tectonics at rest
(that once pushed)

delamination perhaps,
of batholith losing its base—eclogite
holding keel down for heaviness

the mountains, the range,

land to the east
dropping away

I am roaming with history
by volcano's opening
to explosions that blew

laccoliths into distance
rounding the sharpnesses
I feel—

stocks and dikes of rising, striving
to hold their place—
find their escape in surfacing

to breathe
their solidness
from fires reaching
above what is
the mantle.

PLANT

PLANT STRATEGY

It's not the pollinator
but adaptive plant rather

maneuvering sometimes
to secure the transfer

of grains to stigma
down style

(whole pistil) to ovule.
The flower knows

how to make the most
of not just sun and soil

but what's in the middle
of flying around with air

looking for landings
on feasts of color

shades in radiating
spectrum's ultraviolet light.

CIRCUMNUTATION

Plants move
as spirals and irregular curves
around axes unseen,
orbits in air

as in response to gravity
or response to touch

toward stimulus or nastic
change (as in reactive gestures),

or maybe as Darwin had said
endogenous—

internal oscillator
moving plants at cellular level
for driving systems
like tendrils
to convergent evolution
of finding solutions

as in knowing all along
how simply

waveringly
to bend for holding on.

MERISTEM

Meristem in tip and root of plant
is site where cell divides
(undifferentiated)
into one without role,
the other cell programmed
for something more specialized

in plant moving toward transition zone,
propelling itself upwards and down
(through roots and up stem)

meristematic cells with their thin walls
(no vacuoles or barely any at all,
no room for storage of things)

unlike nucleus as reproductive place,
much enlarged, carrying important DNA

for renewal of self
that meeting with transitioning zone

where information (integrated)
will allow for elongation
beyond repairs into new cell growth,

maturations distantly waiting.

SOUNDS OF VIBRATION

Bees know how to buzz
to open their targets'
release of pollen.

Beetles listen for the pop
that indicates a drought
for a tree suffering.

Corn seedling roots
lean towards a sound
like their own,
at 220 Hertz

while chili seedlings
hurry up their growth
if they sense nearby fennel,
the "enemy" they hear,
who slows development
of plant life not their own.

Gas bubbles, too, block the flow
from more air in xylem
turning to embolism
in two-way valves, maybe deadly
the burst, yet pines and Douglas fir
repair damage hourly
when water's lacking.

Plants report impending danger.
True, they warn neighbors
by emitting chemicals.
They share their awarenesses
and are able to respond to touch.

Trees need the wind
to strengthen tissues.

Certain frequencies
increase mullein yields.

Other sounds for other plants
affect metabolism,
even gene mutation.

Plants can drive away their insects
to keep from being eaten—

vegetation's lucky ones.

BOQUILA TRIFOLIOLATA IN CHILEAN RAINFOREST

It's as if you see—
you've eyes—
the way you grow along
woodland floor
to climb to higher radiuses—
transform

how humans don't understand,
they must

disclaim your intelligence
can't explain how
it is your shape gone

your shift in size,
color, veins, orientation—*mimicry*

knowing exactly how much light
you need to stay alive

as in being "stealth vine"
that's what they call you, as if

it's wrong you fear enemies
who would feed off you,

turn your need into toxicity
out of look-alikes in your leaves
that may be

transference of genes from host,
DNA passed through mycorrhizal

into maybe it was airborne chemicals
you knew how to replicate, absorb,

merge into other plant possibilities
of what it is—is a miracle reminding

how we humans don't know—
have yet the full intelligence for—

one after another
beautiful, reaching thing.

QUEEN OF THE ANDES, PUYA RAIMONDII

She defies the odds, monocarpic
shallow roots set down
high unsheltered in Andean Mountains
forming leaf rosette ten feet wide
lined with thorns'
protection of inflorescence towering
into thirty-foot-tall stalk of 30,000
flowers once-in-a-lifetime
emergence from soil's globe of leaves
luring hummingbirds
before six million seeds to fall
by forgotten winds with a trunk
a hundred years needed to bloom,
largest bromeliad,
surviving cold
on rocky slope and standing out
in terrain she has grown from
this far thrust to let go.

ENDANGERED FRISCO CLOVER

You're hanging on with taproot intact,
reddish-purple blooms, shallow ground
among pinion, juniper, sagebrush
spread out, gravel making room
for "invasive" plants to settle
with joining the heavy dust
to pare down seedbanks,
pollination viability,
in these your few areas
of Utah wilderness for growth,
your only home
among miners eroding the earth,
removing the soils,
digging for gold.

MOSS

You are holder of water,
no seed to stem germinating,

neither with roots nor flowers
but rhizoid structures

that thread over objects
to fasten themselves

setting up where
droplets of water
will merge male cells

with female egg, hidden
for fertilization rising
into sporophyte with cap

that when tipped over
will scatter again
birth—several hundred thousand

invitations sent airborne
to willing ground open, waiting.

ANABIOSIS: RETURN TO THE LIVING

In the Karst rocks facing north
off the mountain trail that's been without rain,
you now come alive again to moisture—
bursting thunderhead clouds spilling down
drenching with nourishment.

Ramonda Serbica,
your name asleep a long time—
presumed dead.

Twelve hours for sky's water to revive,
to awaken you on this afternoon in April
with Sun soon to visit with its trail of clouds
and the trills of rock thrush

discoverings of sought-after spring.

REVIVER: FIREWEED

Misnamed
as something unwanted
(as Fire has gone to ash,
got what it came for),
you are the one needed
for replenishing the earth

on patches of scorching,
nitrogen for the taking,
silence for the birthing
your seeds having blown in
for the raising of blooms
upward

over roots' lateral spread
there to nourish the soils
for inviting communities
of life back for refuge
with your faces of lavender
violet, magenta,

your soothing of irritations,
quelling vibrations of disaster,

you are exactly what forests
in their needs will reach for.

FOREST

LODGEPOLE PINE CONE TOUCHED BY FIRE

How long you must wait
for your selves to fall
to the floor of your desires

for meeting
at such a hard-won place
of hidden life changed
into release

of no forest prints or signs
linking animal to plant to life
but soft ash at your feet

now after years
after your Fire sweeps
across your face

with strokes of your arms
again and again licks
with flames of its love

at your fingertip cones
of your grasping
for heat

to your opening
seeds of your birthright
breathing

new ways to down
under the covers of earth

the airs of taking hold
again in darkness to dim

your beginnings, ascent
after Fire has gone
out for fast to slow burning.

THE SILENCING OF FORESTS

Deep-soil water not enough
for Sierra Nevada conifers with
thirst to rising
life sprung from aquifers,

no aquitard stopping
extraction of too much water

evapotranspiration
(leaves cooling themselves)
from heat and draught overbearing

to a drop in water table,
less water reaching streams

signaling rivers depleting.

MOTHER TREE

You are the nurturing hub
connected to hundreds

more trees you send out carbon to,
warnings along with wisdom

to give rise to seedling kin and old neighbors
as your colony draws water and nutrients

from mycorrhizal network
of fungi underground growing threads

to your roots that rocketed you
above the rest,

that gave you height and age,
the moniker of Mother Tree

basking in your tower built toward sun,
filling up with sugars that you need.

You replenish forest in your ancientness,
your laying down important groundwork

for conducting woodland choruses to come
that will take their seats to hum.

THE INTELLIGENCE OF TREES

Trees know what to do
with winter's casting off
leaves from the hormone trigger
(one before several)
to form abscission cells
to push the leaves away from stems,
(leaves' colors changed for protection
from insects and the sun) all
for sending nutrients back
to welcoming bark
through branches down to the trunk
and system of roots. No photosynthesis,
no chlorophyll or respiration in the cold,
no water to climb through
the trees in winter months
(except for some storing H_2O)
when the sun waves its good-byes.
Trees weather scarce times.
They know to wait,
to activate their memory clocks,
minding temperatures and proteins
within themselves, interactions
and old patterns of breaking dormancy
to revive buddings in waiting.
In time each tree will meet again
its bright expected visitor, Spring.

OUTDOOR CONVERSATIONS

Sky and trees touching
to bend light

their branches and boughs
bowing to the earth

as wind blows
softly to a breeze

of uplift and down
the talking whispering

touching there is the forest
of rocks and sounds

all the creatures
outside my doors

beyond my windows
opening wonders.

FAIRY RING FUNGI

Mycelium underneath
mushroom fruit bodies budding from earth.

You are free or tethered (unconnected
or joined with trees). Roots offer nutrients.

You can feed off dead or dying matter,
grow ever outward either way.

At times you kill the grass
or darken greensward from nitrogen release.

Some say they saw the fairies dance,
the circle of so-called destruction

under a full moon of superstition
before their casting of marjoram and thyme,

a little touch of iron. Whether good luck or bad,
the arc you share above ground expands.

TEXTURAL TRIANGLE

Who knew?—not me
of loam's variations.

Like the soil,
I've been in the dark
about a pyramidal structure
released in diagrammatic form
by the
US Department of Agriculture.

Just another fact hidden
somewhere down in my
weighted ignorance.

But a perfect triangle flaunting
percentages of clay, sand, and silt
in determining categories of dirt:

such names as silt loam,
sandy clay, silty clay loam,
or loamy sand, and so they go.

How perfect the angles in the map
of what the earth feels like
and how it appears in admixtures.

I never knew
explanatory triangle existed
to fit the textures of what's below my feet,

reminding me
of mathematical magnificence
touching, holding, the universe.

CREATURE: PART I

THE BLEACHING OF CORAL REEFS, AKA POLYP ANIMALS

Fading color of exoskeletons,
hardened carbonate mineral
of tentacles feeling for—

zooxanthellae you expel,
your partner under water
under sunlight

into the thinning out
marine life not thriving
depending on no longer

the feeding, the spawning,
the nursery grounds, shelter,
these things are gone, going

into fading with forests,
the water's well-meaning
air of seventy-percent

for humans breathing
to suffocation in warming
to the instability of acidity

to the coral reefs of animal
dimming by humans, touch
delivering much to destroy.

HEAD REARRANGEMENT

What made me think
that a mounted head on a wall was okay?
Above the fireplace, remnants of a moose
jut out as if the partial animal belongs there,
its foam-stitched skull screwed together,
glass eyes touched with clay
staring interminably without body, some
tanned, twisted presentation of death, vestige
constructed by taxidermist
as if
stuffed, wild creature seeming to break through wall
at forever-at-peace pace to remind—remind us of what?—
that you, its hunter, killed the animal with a gun?—
How you didn't miss in your shots?
That you scared and delivered pain several times
till the animal lay dead in a blood-spilled no escape?
Maybe someday your own human head
will hang in a home of another alien species,
the trophy of you signifying that your attacker
got you—shot you right in the back—
another easy slaying preserved for all to view—
one more human who didn't see it coming—
clueless you—foraging prey.
You'd proclaim you didn't deserve it—
yet you'd have no voice to call out
to question such an ill-begotten fate.
Your death to silence
would be way beyond your control.

BODACIOUS

What if your name had a so-called prettier ring?
What if instead of Pig you were referred to as . . .
Aurora, Roman Goddess of Sunrise,
some beautiful show of streaming light?

"Pig" suggests dirty, some ugly thing at which to scoff.

It's as if people don't know who you are,
what you can do, how your heart can sing.

With your own kind, you snuggle close,
nose to nose you sleep, taking in everything.

Mother swine, when nursing, you sing to your young.

Piglets answer your calls to them by name.

You eat slowly and not proverbially "like a pig."

And "sweat like a pig" isn't something even possible
since your glands are few.

Being clean is what you prefer; it's in how you live.

You roll in mud for cooling off,
and that's if no water is available.

You are most quick to learn,
your intelligence almost matching apes and dolphins
according to reports. Yet what do humans know?—
cruel species whom you've saved from drowning and fires.

There's much unspoken about the essences
that humans take and make from you:

gelatin for marshmallows, drugs, and photographic film;
ingredients for surgical sutures, industrial lubricants,
explosives, antifreeze, candies and chewing gum,
insulin—more than forty medications;
materials for burn dressings and violin strings;
xenotransplantation, rennet for cheese making,
fatty acid and glycerine for matches,
pig hair for paintbrushes,
pigskin for leather goods; more ingredients
for linoleum, pet food, phonographic records,
pig bone china, drum heads and football coverings,
and on and on the examples

along with your being sacrificed in times of war
as mine sniffers to die for humans.

Yet you, with gestational mystery
of three months, three weeks, three days
before natural timing of birth,

you are Holder of answers, beauty,
inscrutability for awakening the world.

The importance of Pig, Suidae, Sus:

I wish we could let you live.

OPERATION EGGLIFTS

What was it like for you,
tallest of white birds,
as the helicopter flew
down to spill men
out of their whiteness
to pilfer your young
to hatch in two days,
(time frame
when scientists say
you're most protective)

as if you won't notice
one egg gone from two
of clutch

another for white men
preempting offspring

to incubate in drawers

administer oxygen
through tubes
during airline transport,

your chicks later to be
artificially hatched
and raised
with young turkeys,
"pecking bags" for fledglings.

Nineteen born
from "Operation Egglift."

Again no later mating.
Eight years passed

before men charged again
to grab and bend

to artificially inseminate
the bird sperm bank
into your resistance
of no choice airs beating
fear to wildly unknowing
there being no calming first,
no introduction to foreignness,
no gentleness before violation
of space and bodies delicate.

One chick from this—
scientific intervention—
remained alive
seventeen days.

Humans returned
for gatherings, more eggs
Northwest Territories
(whooping crane attachments)
embryonic-stage

plunder for delivery
to Gray's Lake, Idaho nests
of sandhill cranes
(their own eggs removed
for artificial birthing),

National Wildlife Refuge
name not protecting.

Some nine "whoopers"
hatched—shaped
into same story
setting of no blessing:

Birds never bred:
Experiment terminated.

Birds decimated,
almost the extinction
around 1940

to become lands overrun
beyond the guns of humans
still to this day exerting
as controlling hands of centuries.

ICE ECOREGIONS: REFLECTIONS OF WHITE BEAR

Polar bear top of the world
Rolling down on back to side
Bank of body of seas to sleep
Marble blue swirl into landscape

Moon-dream craters, plateaus,
Sea ice, floes,
Leads and polynyas,
Waters of cold, Bears

Daring to go inland
Arctic their world
For disappearing

Further their swimming
To melting of no reach

Like guard hairs of hollow,
Scattering of light,

Visible wavelengths
Rippling

CREATURE: PART II

FOOTPRINTS, BOBCAT, FRESH SNOW

I visit these woods,
stranger to a foreign land
of conifers (juniper
and pine)

the currants, manzanita,
snowbrush and boulders
holding to the earth

and being held
one and the same
this network
of connections

of tracks I follow
in snow to let go,
to never step too far with,

I only want to be close to
breath in the cold,
the stillness, aloneness

of how the animal chooses
its range of solitude

I want to be a part of

keeping the distance,

holding wildness close.

BIRDS AT BAYSIDE

How perfect the balance of
countercurrent
heat exchanger in winter's gull
as it keeps her feet from cooling
to a frostbite. Intertwining
arteries and veins regulate
temperature to where bird's feet
stay cool yet warm enough,
her legs working around the clock
to keep her life from harm.

CHICKADEE

I scooped her up
thinking she was dead,
or would die soon in my hand,
having flown out at me
to meet her impact other side of me
unexpected hardness before a fall.
The flutters, spasms,
talons curled under
twisted her toward a death
where breath was labored,
her softness pulsing the aches
of terror to the unfamiliar,
I could only imagine.
I wanted to somehow calm
whatever was passing
as her thin eye film closed
to her struggle lessening
from where, it seemed,
she refused departure,
or else could not yet move.
I tried setting her down,
but she stayed to settle
in the cup of my hand
for minutes I remained . . .
until she looked about
as if to sense or touch
familiars.
I waited, made sounds

that I hoped would comfort.
Then blinks came,
the unfolding of claws,
the shaking out of wings,
her captured state a release
of coming into herself
in a way most different . . .
She looked at me then
alert, with starts and turns,
to right herself again
toward Earth and sky;
and for herself
with uplifted heart—
set off to fly.

CRAB SHELLS

Even hermits lose their homes,
outgrow their shells

for crabs to line up in single file ritual,
the biggest to the smallest crab
in their normal housing exchange,
hoping for a swap
and another shell's arrival.
(New homes tried on for easy size.)

With one crab left
out from the shuffle,
she finds a mackerel
tin can nearby instead

to squeeze herself into
for dragging around new metal.

It all works out for now,
this new yet old
exoskeleton cylinder.

BUTTERFLY

Compound eyes
provide widest visual range
in animal and insect kingdom,

almost as if each orb
sees all the way around itself—

with ultraviolet light as friend

to butterfly that holds such light
close to itself, maybe to become one
with a certain band in purple spectrum

in winged one's search for food
and potential mates, and for homing in
on nectars and cues of blossoms
in colors signaling pollination viability,

while in other ways UV light
serves butterfly as protection—

as in lit, patterned disguise
on wings against predators.

BROTHERHOOD

No brewer's blackbird in the lavender
but a brotherhood of cowbirds' oratorio of feasting
on a stump with seeds and cracked corn
celebration as they raise their backs and heads,
puff out breasts, spread their tails, lift their wings,
and bow
again   and again   and again.

ELEPHANT SISTERHOOD

In the center of fanfare
stands the newly born
elephant calf
working to stay upright
with the help of females
(losing control
of bodies in celebrating)
and mother's rumble
of trunk lending support
for new life, savanna
now in Rhodes
and red oat grass
under tropical
acacia tree canopy
appearing blown away
by trumpetings
over plain
of elephant herd
flappings of ears
raising of tails
turning themselves
into guardian
spinner of dreams—
givers and keepers—
roarings, elephant love.

MIGRATION

DIEL VERTICAL MIGRATION

Out for tasting of night,
copepods and larvae,
barnacles and anemones,
starfish and pelagic worms—

these and more
than ten thousand species
of zooplankton make for
(in microscopic terms)

largest of animal migration
around the globe
(freshwater or ocean)—

bodies that rise with their wake
from the deep in their meeting
orchestration of drifters,
while avoiding the light,

dimming predation, reaching
for first chain in life, marine
giver of breath for all the Earth,
that plant of bloom, that surface

dweller of ornamentation,
developer of carbon sink,
diatoms, coccolithophores—
designs, some of dream

turning from chalky white
to streams of blue
swirling back a sky,

or filigrees turned edible
shells of glass into gold

MIGRATIONS OF SEA TURTLES

For thousands of miles
having migrated,
soon-to-be mother sea turtles

I marvel at how long you've lived
through chances of survival
being less than one percent.

Magnetic mineral particles
within must be what orients
towards Earth's magnetic field.

You find your way home again
to places of your birth
for the laying of your clutch

in sands of beach protection, nests
for covering the young, those
who will soon set off for night—

hatchlings towards unknown light—
presumed haven that might just be
their distant, guiding moon.

RED CRAB MIGRATION

First rainfall's cavalcade:
One hundred and twenty million
crabs scuttle from forests at same time
to mate and spawn at Indian Ocean,
Christmas Island, Australia.

A hundred thousand eggs fill a brood pouch.
Always the release of eggs before dawn
on receding high tide, last quarter moon,
with mothers' pinchers raised high in the air.

Larvae hatch at first contact with water
to mostly perish in a world not for saving
as the tide carries them out to sea,
and maybe in days later to surface
an offering back to the earth as gift—
baby crabs—a place for hidden safety.

PACIFIC SALMON RUN

You are programmed for your end
(phenoptosis as the scientists say)
as you swim Pacific waters home
for the rivers of your becoming

first alevin to parr then smolt,
freshwater, brackish, to ocean
of your adulthood in your knowing
you must go back for scent pulling

perhaps with Earth's magnetic field
to anadromous, the thousands of miles
of days and temperatures, environment
triggering timings for birth

alongside passings with exaction,
surrenderings into sacrifice, desired
the head hump jaw teeth growing
in males for the fight of protection

you are swimming upstream, female
and male at mountains of waterfalls
forging into what you must to move
your life to its fading of red

to the paling into ghosts of flesh,
parts of you removed, fallen
disintegration to spread
after the laying of labors
down the fanned gravel of eggs—

continuity of life, riverbed
of oxygen and depth, underwater
quiverings, upwellings—everything
elemental, your returnings to Earth.

MIGRATION: MONARCH BUTTERFLY

Imagine Super Generation—
travelers of 45 hundred miles
down the continental U.S.
from Canada into Mexico
for a place of never been to,

this 5th generation stronger,
larger, living eight times longer
for the farthest of flyings
filled with sweet nectar, pollen,
reserves after diapause

with an inborn compass (solar)
and antennas telling time,
magnetosensors, other tool
for polarization of light
as they ride the thermals,

these butterflies in migration
for pine and oak forests
in Michoacán, Mexico,
places of never been to,
yet always the same

these sites for overwintering,
for their covering of trees,
arriving before the honoring
Day of the Dead,
as in winged spirits revisiting

to be warmed for months
huddling in their know
what they want, this is their time
of regeneration for journey
that won't return them home

but will take them north
to the milkweed of southern states,
for drumming of leaves of scent
knowing they're in the landing
of right place birthing spring.

REPOSE

October meets butterflies'
linger in their tortoiseshell design

familiar by the hundreds
alongside spring water
near the trail on which I'm walking, as if

they rest after earlier spring's call,
annual migration to mate
toward the laying down of eggs
in tobacco brush, snow brush, hidden.

It won't be long before they'll hibernate,
leave for lower elevation.

They have their patterns.
Open and close,
open and close.

Their wings convey a sign
before lifting off again
toward rivers of fluttering skies.

MIGRATORY FLIGHT OF THE BAR-TAILED GODWIT

For eight days you journey
seventy-two hundred miles straight—
thirty-five miles an hour—flock
with no rest, food, or water—
nothing for your nourishing
high above Pacific Ocean
within gusts and storms,
cyclones pummeling
to the trade winds pulling
you strive to
stay the course so far
to your island of New Zealand,
(accompanied by your young
no longer the fledglings)
to travel following yearly cycle
of breeding and birth, life
over Alaskan tundra
and the feeding-filling with clams
and worms, seeds and berries
to double in size your weight
for the journey to shrink
your insides from working,
(to make room for fat),
the necessary shut-down
(partial) of your delicate brain
into conserving energy, strategies
(biological) maintaining

what you must
for arriving at distant destination
days after your Alaskan calls
you made resounding
met with preening,
bathing, stretching towards leading
from water's edge wading
you lift yourselves one by one
into finding known V formation
in a flight drawing you into skies and wind
inviting the letting go.

MIRACLES, MORE

WATER BEARS

For over 500 million years
through five mass extinctions,
tardigrades have made their homes:

in volcanos and Himalayas,
at pressures six times greater
than Mariana's Trench floor,

and in space and temperatures
from minus 273 degrees
to 150 degrees Celsius.

They've survived radiation
one thousand times greater
than what humans withstand.

They've gone without food
for thirty years and floated around
without air until found again.

They make ice crystallize within
to protect themselves from expansion
and release their water if needed
to turn into a ball and dry out dormant.

They make large amounts of antioxidants,
with still more tricks and mysteries
for defying all the odds, these creatures

much adept at prolonging for years
their lives
intended only for weeks.

DMS

Phytoplankton carry you
away to cloud formation.

You are sulfur molecule,
two added methyl groups.

You are distinctive smell
picked by marine life and birds

for finding what attracts.
Without you,

sunlight would not reflect
back into space. Sulfur

aerosols must join with water,
needing air that goes

from gas to liquid
to shapes in a sky

of meanings, forever
changing human reflections.

IMMORTALITY

Hydra,
how do you stay the same?
No senescence, no loss in fertility,
you are out to bud, regenerate,
grow two heads if you must
if your fibers cross.

You just go on and on,
stem cells refreshing.

Reproducing
sexually or not,
you come from parent sponge.

Prokaryote can live inside you
to eat what you don't want
and spit out what it is you crave.

You rip apart for sustenance,
a miracle for such a small thing.

FRACTAL REMINDERS

Chaotic equations moved you
from turbulence
to duplicative patterns.
Everywhere I look or imagine,
I should find you in reflections:
clouds and nervous system,
the edges of Saturn's rings,
mountain ranges, lightning bolts,
seashells and coast lines, crystals,
and waterfalls. You are here to stay,
finite in area, perimeter ad infinitum.

FIBONACCI SERIES FROM INDIAN MATHEMATICIANS

The petals of flowers remind
of Fibonacci numbers, the sequence
of which leads to *golden ratio*.

Spirals reflect numbers universally
in seed heads, pinecones, leaf arrangements,
sea life, vegetables, spiral galaxies,
fruit, human measurements,
art, theology

(notwithstanding exceptions)
there are yet more signs of phi—
the length of a song times .618
to equal climax point
for listeners
to follow
the universe guiding
moments of completion,

the satiety of humans
in their life that's a curve
(maybe a *golden spiral*)
each color a wavelength
and frequency,
divine proportion,
these squares, rectangles,
and circles all with

something the same
overarching for signaling
what's considered *irrational*,
untranslatable, without fractions,
no one thing overpowering another.

HEMIMASTIGOTE (AKA HAIRY, RAPACIOUS OGRE)

Flagella-waving look-alike raisin—
yet no cartoon animation
as you stand supra-kingdom
beyond complex categories
of known forms of life—

plant and animal,
fungus, protozoan and now one more addition
in the eukaryotic life—

you went renegade as microbe
over a billion years ago, unnoticed
branch in the tree of life.

Your existence is now confirmed.

Yes, we humans can be slow to catch on,
blind to what's beneath our feet
or before our vision.

So now I wonder,
have to admit—how much more
can be uncovered

right between my very toes?

SUBTERRANEAN BIOSPHERE

Fifteen to twenty-three billion tons—
static microorganisms
yet some extant thousands of years
in ecosystem twice the size
of all the world's oceans.

Extraterrestrial
methanogen
to produce methane,
to replace or repair
broken parts of itself.

And geogemma barossii,
once classified as bacteria
and occupying vents
at hydrothermal spot
on ocean floor to reproduce
at 121° centigrade.

Five thousand meters below ground,
life forms apart from the sun to survive,
to thrive on pressure and little nutrients.

Humans find answers during exploration
of core covered over to inverted life
mushrooming down,
spreading earth cloud.

OUTER SPACE

GOLDEN NEBULA

We move into Light—Photon Belt,
electromagnetic cloud—

electrons and positrons
annihilate themselves
on course for collision.

Photon Band orbits Pleiades.

Alcyone and Galactic Core
stream waves—energy increase—

conjunction
again after 26,000 years

our solar system
having orbited Alcyone
and Milky Way,

where now we enter
awaited *Golden Nebula*,

here two thousand more years.

ARMS OF THE MILKY WAY HOLDING STARS

Trillions of galaxies surround the arms,
galaxies not consumed by ours
beyond the dark matter,
beyond our halo, our globular clusters.
Young massive stars brighten spirals,
having been born from nebulae
(clouds of gas and dust)
that collapse and collide—stars
webbed by arms' gravity.
Density waves (another name
for curved rays of Milky Way),
formed from molecular clouds
of hydrogen. A living body,
they do not stay the same.
Stars and gas accelerate
towards them before
slowing and entering,
before moving away
in orbit or fading
from arms' embrace
into dwarf stars,
or maybe, maybe
into lives of
supernovae.

MILKY WAY'S BLACK HOLE

It's the mass that draws us in, black hole
that awaits stars and gas clouds
with a gravitational pull
not even light can escape.

The dark emits high energy particles
as breath from vortex magnitude.

Fourteen million miles across
(opposed by magnetic fields),
black hole
of galactic core
still cannot take in

everything.
Expulsion of matter occurs.

STAR CONSUMED

Black hole swallowed star,

Swift drawing close, a gas
to form accretion disk
millions of degrees hot.

Jets drove particles out
almost at the speed of light—
(powered by magnetic fields)
to be flares lasting years
as X-ray, gamma, ultraviolet

taking 3.9 billion years
to reach Earth, with X-rays
10,000 times brighter
than what's normal
for known tidal disruptions
of a black hole, cavern
one million times more
than the mass of the sun.

They say a star was shredded.
I think more it was gifted
new light, a burst of energy

beaming
funnels opposite direction travel,
cosmic rays birthed—
fastest known particles.

NEUTRON STAR REVIVED

Solar winds remove the red
giant star's outer layers

as magnetic field
of smaller star companion
in shared orbit around
common center

still keeps going strong
in defying death,
in being somehow young

and provided nourishment
(transfer of mass
from red giant star
gravitationally bound)

leading up to
unheard of
bursts of

X-ray light
on neutron star:
solar winds' offering

a blanket
over presumed core

of prolonged passing.

BINARY SYSTEM: WHITE DWARF ACCOMPANYING RED GIANT

Collapse to fragment in cloud of gas.
Interstellar clumps form the birth of stars
touched by dust, some bound by gravitation
to orbit around a common center. If closer,
stars transfer mass, meaning one grows
while the other (white dwarf)
pulls in matter forming a disk
around its body. Nova burst
of brightness might happen,
or a largening into a hot red giant
losing its outer shell of gas
in explosion ejection of mass—
as brightest supernova
to pass into neutrons, a star—
maybe into a pulsar
or into the making of
another galactic black hole.

REFLECTION NEBULA

You are interstellar dust
reflecting light,

grains of micron
size
containing silicates,
aluminum oxide,
calcium, hydrogen.

You are where stars are born,
unlike your sisters, your brethren
of supernovae remnants
or planetary nebulae
that encircle stars dying.

You are the blue that scatters,
the dust that covers,
the motion of magnetic fields,

holders and flyers
of impermanence,

galactic dazzle
unreachable.

DARK MATTER

You bend Light passing by,
cavort with Gravity,
who likes the creation of new space
everywhere,
energy building,

universe expanding,
accelerating

as hydrogen learned to separate,
to cool down
from your closeness,

to form stars of its own,
small galaxies in a universe
of 85% no emission,
no absorption of light.

Like dark energy invisible,
you pass right through us
knowing
all along you belong to Mystery.

ACKNOWLEDGMENTS

With much gratitude to the following publishers:

All-Creatures.org: Elephant Sisterhood; The Bleaching of Coral Reefs, AKA Polyp Animals

Anthology Forest: book anthology: The Silencing of Forests (poem reprint)

Audubon Alaska: (first appeared): Chickadee

Becoming-Feral: book anthology: Bodacious (poem reprint)

Botany of Gaia: book anthology, reprints: Elephant Sisterhood, Migrations of Sea Turtles

Earth Lines: Geopoetry and Geopoetics: book anthology: Tor, Scree

Environ Monitor: Repose (poem reprint)

Interalia Magazine: The Intelligence of Trees, Hemimastigote (AKA Hairy, Rapacious Ogre), Fairy Ring Fungi, Mother Tree, Subterranean Biosphere, Sounds of Vibration, Immortality, Arms of the Milky Way Holding Stars, Textural Triangle, Lodgepole Pine Cone Touched by Fire, Circumnutation, Meristem, Fractal Reminders, Fibonacci Series from Indian Mathematicians, DMS, Dark Matter, Reflection Nebula, Star Consumed

Journal for Critical Animal Studies: Operation Egglifts, Bodacious

Nebo: A Literary Journal: Head Rearrangement

Not Very Quiet: Boquila Trifoliolata in Chilean Rainforest

Plants & Poetry Journal: Anabiosis: Return to the Living, Plant Strategy

Plum Tree Tavern: Endangered Frisco Clover, Brotherhood

Red Planet Magazine: Binary System: White Dwarf Accompanying Red Giant, Neutron Star Revived, Milky Way's Black Hole

Rising Moon Healing Center Newsletter: Golden Nebula

Stravaig #9: Mountain Ice: Snow Pack

Stravaig #11: Sierra Nevada: Volcanic Arc, Inactive Subduction Zone (poem reprint); Anabiosis: Return to the Living (poem reprint)

The Environmental Magazine: Water Bears; Migratory Flight of the Bar-Tailed Godwit; Red Crab Migration; Migration of Sea Turtles; Pacific Salmon Run; Repose; Footprints, Bobcat, Fresh Snow; Migration: Monarch Butterfly; Ice Ecoregions: Reflections of White Bear; Diel Vertical Migration; Sierra Nevada: Volcanic Arc, Inactive Subduction Zone

Thimble Literary Magazine: Queen of the Andes, Puya Raimondii

Tiny Seed Literary Journal: Butterfly, Moss, Reviver Fireweed, Outdoor Conversations, Birds at Bayside, The Silencing of Forests

Triangulation: Habitat: book anthology: Crab Shells

LIST OF ABBREVIATIONS

AKA in poem title stands for "also known as"

DNA is an abbreviation for deoxyribonucleic acid

DMS stands for the gas dimethylsulfide, which plays a big part in regulating climate

www.ingramcontent.com/pod-product-compliance
Lightning Source LLC
Chambersburg PA
CBHW070302100426
42743CB00011B/2314